I0797856

A MOMENT IN TIME

A MOMENT IN TIME

DESIGNING A COUNTRY GARDEN

KATHRYN HERMAN

New York · Paris · London · Milan

CONTENTS

FOREWORD

Much of the inspiration for the gardens I've created here has come from my travels—journeys far and wide across the globe, with the gardens of England serving as the most profound influence. There is something about the way English gardens blend tradition with innovation, structure with wildness, that has always captured my imagination. From the perfectly groomed lines of the formal gardens to the unruly beauty of the cottage-style borders, I have been shaped by the vast variety of landscapes that this country offers. But of all the experiences that have shaped my work, none have had as lasting an impact as my time spent at Hadspen House.

Years before I even considered designing gardens myself, I had the privilege of spending a week at Hadspen House under the mentorship of the incomparable Penelope Hobhouse. At the time, the garden was managed by Nori and Sandra Pope, whose work would become some of the most influential in my life. The week was a mixture of lectures, garden visits, and ample free time to wander through the garden itself, and it was during those unstructured hours that I was able to soak in the magic of the place.

The experience at Hadspen was transformative. There was something almost alchemical about the way the borders were planted, the way colors and textures seamlessly melded into one another. I was struck by the ethereal combinations—blues blending into purples, yellows fading into soft pinks, all with a graceful ease that made it appear as though the plants had naturally grown together over time. But as I walked through those borders, I realized this wasn't an accident; it was the result of careful thought, attention to detail, and a deep understanding of color. The Popes' approach was revolutionary in its precision. I began to see color not as a random burst but as a tool to craft emotion, mood, and movement within a garden.

Before that week, I had appreciated color in the garden, but my understanding of it had been superficial. Hadspen showed me that color could tell a story—that it could elevate a simple planting into something extraordinary. It wasn't enough to use any plant in any color. There was a harmony to be achieved, a specific shade to be found, and the result was nothing short of enchanting. I remember feeling both awestruck and inspired. It made me rethink the way I approached my own plantings and forced me to ask myself what I wanted my gardens to communicate.

When I returned home, I couldn't wait to dive deeper into this new world of color. I immediately added *Colour by Design*, the Popes' influential book, to my library. That book became my bible. The way they articulated the relationship between color and design, how they curated plant combinations that spoke to each other rather than clashed, was revolutionary. I became obsessive about finding those perfect shades, the plants that would provide not just color, but the right color, in the right context.

One of the first major projects I took on after that experience was designing a herbaceous border, and it was here that I truly put what I had learned to the test. I remember going through the plant catalogs, looking for plants that could be carefully selected to work together—not just in terms of form and texture, but in terms of their color palette. It was clear that a border wasn't simply about variety but about cohesion, about blending hues that would complement one another in ways that felt intentional and subtle, not jarring or accidental.

Hadspen House taught me that a garden should never be static. It should always be evolving, always moving, always changing in subtle ways. The borders at Hadspen were perfect examples of this philosophy. Every time I walked through them, there was something new to discover. The plants were constantly shifting, with each season bringing a new combination of color, texture, and form. That sense of constant change is something I strive for in my own gardens—though, of course, the challenges of designing for New England's short season are a far cry from those of the temperate English climate.

Still, the influence of that week in England continues to shape how I design. When I look at the garden now, I can see the fingerprints of those early lessons. I see the careful planning, the exacting shades of color that create harmony, and the way the plants work together, never competing but instead enhancing one another. The herbaceous borders that I've designed here owe much to that week at Hadspen, and every time I step into one of those spaces, I am reminded of how deeply that experience influenced my journey.

But it wasn't just the planting combinations that stayed with me; it was also the philosophy behind it all. The gardens I visited, the ones that left a lasting impact, weren't just beautiful; they were thoughtful, intentional, and always in dialogue with their surroundings. They didn't just exist as static works of art; they were living, breathing spaces that invited visitors to engage, to explore, and to learn. And in this, they were more than just gardens—they were experiences.

My travels—especially in England—taught me that a garden is not just a collection of plants, but a place waiting to be discovered. They showed me that a garden should be designed not just for the seasons, but for the soul. Each time I take a step into the garden now, I do so with that same sense of curiosity, that same awe for the way plants, color, and design can come together to create something far greater than the sum of its parts.

Hadspen House, with its bold, inventive use of color and its thoughtful design, was a moment of clarity for me. It helped me understand that a garden can be a place where beauty isn't just seen but felt, where each plant, each color, each texture plays a part in telling a larger story. And every garden I've designed since that week has been informed by that story—one that continues to evolve, one that has no end, and one that will keep influencing my work for years to come.

Overleaf: A view of the motor court and house. The eight *Taxus baccata* 'Hicksii' were planted a hundred years ago; they once served as plantings in front of the eight stall stables, which burned down in 1997, and now act as a backdrop and connection between the house and garage.

CHAPTER ONE

HISTORY

The story of my garden doesn't really begin with me, but rather with Margaret and Henry Rudkin. They married in 1923 and, by 1926, had purchased 125 acres of land in Fairfield, Connecticut, where they set out to create a gentleman's farm. Margaret, who had studied math and finance and worked in banking and brokerage, and Henry, a successful Wall Street broker, both sought the adventure of farming and raising their own livestock. Though part of the property had once been a farm, the Rudkins built a house and various outbuildings to support their new agrarian lifestyle. They named their estate Pepperidge Farm, inspired by the large *Nyssa sylvatica* trees on the property, known as blackgum, black tupelo, or sour gum.

To design their new home and buildings, the Rudkins hired architect Walter Bradnee Kirby, who at the time ran his own office in New York City. He designed a house, a garage with an apartment above, a grooms' cottage, stables, and a gamecock house. The buildings were constructed between 1928 and 1929. Surrounding the house and farm buildings was an orchard of five hundred apple trees. The garage, which originally had nine bays for automobiles, also included a six-by-ten-foot freezer room for storing beef and pork raised on the property.

Margaret and Henry had three sons: Henry A. Rudkin, Jr. (1924–2008), William Lincoln Rudkin Sr. (1926–2013), and John Mark Rudkin (1929–2019). The garden begins with the architecture. In my case, it all starts with a 1928 groom's cottage, designed by Kirby. He had trained at MIT and graduated in the class of 1907. He went on to study at the American Academy in Rome in 1911 and traveled and studied throughout Europe in 1912. He later worked as a draftsman for several renowned architects before joining the landscape architectural firm Vitale, Brinckerhoff & Geiffert in 1915.

Opposite, above: The *Nyssa sylvatica*, or pepperidge tree, at left, is the tree from which the property takes its name.

Opposite, below: One of the company's original bread delivery trucks.

PEPPERIDGE FARM BREAD

PEPPERIDGE FARM BREAD
MADE AT PEPPERIDGE FARM IN FAIRFIELD, CONN.

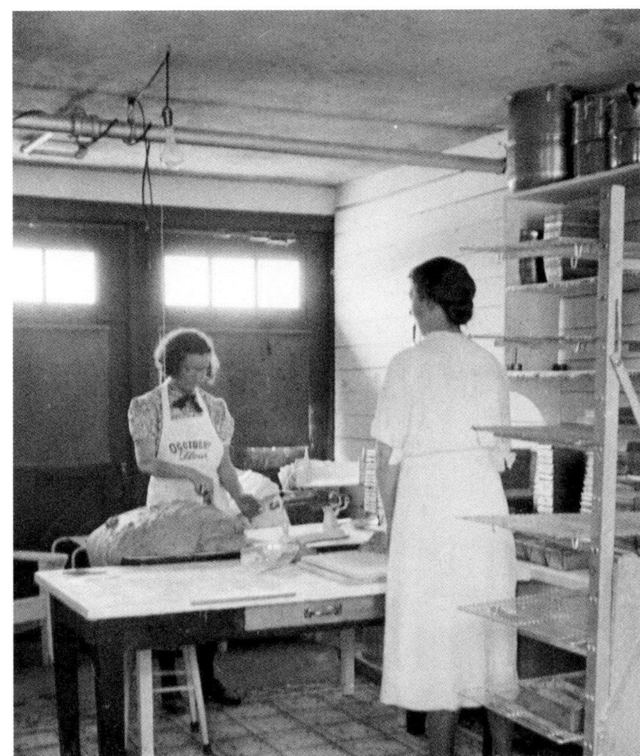

In the garden's creation, I must mention Agnes Selkirk Clark (1898–1983), a notable landscape architect. Agnes attended the Lowthorpe School of Landscape Architecture from 1915 to 1918 and worked for various firms, including Pearse & Robinson in Des Moines, Iowa, and Ellen Biddle Shipman in New York. In 1921, she married architect Charles Cameron Clark, and together they moved to Fairfield, where Agnes designed the gardens off the main house terrace. She filled the formal garden with lilacs, azaleas, peonies, tulips, and lilies, bordered by *Iberis sempervirens*, creating a picturesque space that still resonates today.

While Margaret Rudkin had a passion for flowers, Henry was particularly knowledgeable about trees and shrubs. This love of plants was passed down, especially to Mark, the youngest brother, who became a renowned garden designer. Mark received commissions in France for the Musée d'Art Américain in Giverny, a garden at the Palais Royal in Paris, and a garden for the Franco-American Museum at Château de Blérancourt in Picardy. His own garden, Le Bois du Fay, in Le Mesnil-Saint-Denis, was also a celebrated creation.

In 1937, when Mark was nine years old and struggling with asthma and allergies, Margaret took it upon herself to bake fresh, homemade bread for him. She sold it at a local market, Mercurio's, and always made sure to give Mark's allergist a loaf to try. Eventually, she approached Charles & Co., a specialty grocer, and they agreed to take twenty-four loaves a day. The bread was baked in the converted garage. The December 1939 issue of *Reader's Digest* even published an article titled "Bread, de Luxe" by J.D. Ratcliff.

By 1940, the baking operation moved from the garage into the converted stables, and later, into a purpose-built factory in Norwalk, Connecticut, also designed by Walter Bradnee Kirby. The factory was designed in a U shape, allowing ingredients to be received at one end and finished products shipped out at the other.

The property itself, originally a gentleman's farm, underwent changes over time. As the need for space grew, the grooms' cottage, caretaker's apartment, garage, and gamecock house were subdivided from the main house and property. As its new owner, I have since worked to breathe new life into these structures, adding new garden spaces and plantings while restoring historical hedging and topiaries. This work respects the original architectural intentions and maintains the integrity of the property's past.

Through these transitions, the garden and its buildings continue to tell the story of this place, combining history, architecture, and nature in ways that honor the original vision of Margaret and Henry Rudkin.

Opposite, top: Loading up bread for delivery in front of the garage and stables.

Opposite, bottom left: Portrait of Margaret Rudkin, founder of Pepperidge Farm.

Opposite, bottom right: Many of Margaret's employees were women from the neighborhood. Here they are weighing out dough in the garage, which was converted into a bread-baking facility.

Right: In spring, the weeping cherries are in full glory. Sprays of soft pink flowers occur before leaves emerge, giving the impression that the trees are covered by snow.

Overleaf: The south façade of the 1928 groom's cottage. The half-timbered, stone-and-clapboard cottage once housed the grooms who cared for the horses that lived in the stables. The slope is planted with no-mow fescue grass and bordered by a boxwood hedge. Two types of ivy (*Parthenocissus tricuspidata* and *Helix hedera Helix hedera*) soften the stone façade. Monolithic slabs of bluestone connect the front terrace to the grounds.

Above: The house's foundation is surrounded by a low boxwood hedge that acts like a datum around the entire building. *Parthenocissus tricuspidata* softens the stone façade.

Right: Two oak-and-metal planters demarcate the front entry, each filled with a single boxwood. The no-mow fescue grass slope is backed by a boxwood hedge and a *Rosa multiflora*.

Overleaf: Early morning light streams through the house and out over the western façade. Boxwoods shaped into domed squares echo the axis from the house to the landscape. An *Ulmus americana* towers over the house and provides shade from the sometimes intense late-afternoon sun.

A fieldstone wall surrounds the sunken pool garden. Wisteria, Zephirine Drouhin roses, honeysuckle, and clematis all grow along and over the stones.

Above: A re-creation of the original gate is fitted between the two stone piers. Freshly sheared *Ligustrum ovalifolium* completes the motor court's enclosure.

Right: Opposite view of the sheared privet hedge, showing the *Taxus baccata* 'Hicksii' "muffins" and flowering *Cornus kousa* behind.

Overleaf: Originally built as a nine-car garage with a three-bedroom apartment, this building has served many functions over the decades, including as a home for the caretakers, a bakery, and offices. A large *Quercus palustris* grows behind.

A view into the pool garden. The pool measures 12 by 24 feet, mirroring the dimensions of the original gamecock house, now a dining pavilion. Three-inch-thick, rock-faced bluestone coping edges the pool, which is finished in a French gray plaster.

Left: The garage as seen from the meadow. The area is anchored by a *Magnolia* x *soulangeana*, chosen for its form and soft pink blossoms, which work well against the brown of the building.

Overleaf: Custom gates along the road allow access for larger equipment. The boxwood squares are set beyond one of the surviving apple trees; at one time, 400 of them covered the property's original 125 acres.

HEDGING

Of all the plants that grace the property, there is one that stands out as particularly unique and special—the yew muffins. These *Taxus baccata* 'Hicksii'—known simply as yews—have an almost magical quality to them. Long-lived and endlessly adaptable, yews are capable of regenerating growth even after being pruned, and they can take on almost any shape, which is part of their charm. With their dark, rich green foliage, they stand as both sentinels and sculptural forms, quietly commanding the landscape.

The yew muffins are not just any shrubs. They are living pieces of history. Eight of them were planted around 1928, just outside the original stables, to demarcate the stalls' patterning. The double pair, sitting on axis with both the main door to the stables and the main door of the house, are part of a thoughtful alignment that remains to this day. These yews have weathered almost a century of changes, their form preserved, their purpose unchanged. And while many of the original structures have come and gone—the stables themselves were lost to fire in 1997—the yews stand as steadfast witnesses to the passage of time.

They have a unique beauty, especially when sheared in late summer after the heat has passed. This is when their intricate domed forms really shine, giving the garden a sense of whimsy and scale. The fact that these trees have been here for nearly a hundred years only adds to their significance. They are not just plants; they are legacy, living links to the past, and guardians of a garden that has withstood the test of time.

But winter—winter is the true test of any garden. Gone are the flowers, the leaves, the fragrance that distract from the bare bones of the landscape. What remains must stand on its own, stripped of the seasonal adornments that fill the warmer months. And here, in the dead of winter, the yews come into their own. Snow gathers on their rounded, sculptural forms, softening their edges, turning them into gentle, living sculptures against a backdrop of white. These yews hold their shape through the coldest months, never faltering, offering a touch of life when everything else seems to have faded away.

Winter in New England, particularly, is a time of reflection. Our long, seemingly endless winters challenge the garden in ways that the other seasons do not. Half of the year, we are covered in snow, the landscape turned quiet and dormant. In the absence of blossoms and the full foliage of summer, the garden must reveal itself through its bones—the structure of the landscape, the evergreens, the silhouettes of trees and shrubs.

In my mind, the mark of a truly great garden is its ability to offer interest even in the dead of winter. When the vibrant colors of spring and summer are gone, the garden should still speak to you. The yews, in particular, stand as a testament to this. They hold their shape, their structure, and in doing so, they continue to contribute to the garden's design long after the last bloom has faded.

The bones of the garden—those structural elements like yews, boxwoods, and hedges—become the focus in winter. When all else is stripped away, the garden transforms into something minimalist, almost abstract. There is beauty in this simplicity, in the way the forms of the plants and trees are exposed. Without the distractions of flowers or leaves, the garden becomes more about shape, about the lines that guide the eye, and about the way light falls across the surfaces.

I am fortunate to live in a part of the world where stone walls, remnants of our farming heritage, are also a defining feature of the landscape. These walls, built by hand generations ago, take on an entirely new form under the snow. They undulate and snake their way through the woods, their contours softened by the blanket of white. They become a study in texture and form, understated and yet so important to the character of the property.

But if stone walls alone aren't enough to provide the structure and form that winter demands, there are plenty of plants that can rise to the occasion. One of my personal favorites is the *Fagus sylvatica*, or beech. With its fawn-colored autumn leaves clinging to its branches through much of the winter, it adds a subtle, yet striking, warmth to the cold landscape. Likewise, *Carpinus betulus* (hornbeam) also holds its

Opposite: Bright-green, fresh growth covers the yew in spring.

leaves into the winter months, creating a delicate, golden veil against the backdrop of snow. Both trees, when planted as hedges, create a sense of enclosure, drawing the eye into the space they define.

Privet, though I sometimes refer to it as the "summer holiday weekend shrub," is another excellent option for a structured winter garden. It requires regular pruning—around Memorial Day, the Fourth of July, and Labor Day—to keep it in top form, but it rewards you with a dense, upright growth that can be sheared into neat, sculpted forms.

Boxwood is another favorite of mine, especially in the winter months when its dense, evergreen foliage stands as a pillar of structure. Boxwoods can be planted in neat hedges or allowed to grow into more billowy, rounded forms. In winter, when all other plants have been stripped bare, they take on a new role—creating negative space, their shape defined by the absence of everything else. There is something magical about a row of snow-covered boxwoods, their rounded forms blanketed in white, their presence still holding weight in the garden even as everything else is hidden under the frost.

Of course, the yews are the gold standard when it comes to evergreen form. Yews, in particular, can be shaped into almost any imaginable form, making them a versatile addition to the winter garden. Whether as a hedge or a topiary, yews offer endless possibilities. In fact, I've often encouraged others not to be afraid to think outside the box when it comes to using yews. Why not create a curving, serpentine hedge that winds its way through your property, or imagine a mass of different-sized balls of boxwood, all dusted with snow? There is no need for formality or rigidity in the garden. Sometimes, the most beautiful forms come from allowing plants to evolve and express themselves in unexpected ways.

Opposite: Summer sun invites a close perusal of the sharply toothed leaves of a hornbeam (*Carpinus betulus*).

Opposite: Winter allows for the underlying form of plants to stand out. The domed tops of the *Taxus* are highlighted by a dusting of snow, while the *Fagus sylvatica* hedge shows off its tawny winter color and rectilinear form.

Above: *Carpinus betulus* is a marcescent species, meaning it holds its leaves throughout winter.

Overleaf: The horizontal line of the *Taxus baccata* 'Hicksii' hedge that surrounds the vegetable garden is broken by four Braeburn apple trees.

CHAPTER TWO

THE PERENNIAL GARDEN

My love for plants has always been a central part of my life. It's a passion that began long before I started designing gardens, and one that continues to shape my work today. This love was sparked by my early experiences with plants and cultivated through years of exploration and study. As a child, I didn't fully realize how deep my connection to nature ran, but over time, I found myself constantly drawn to the beauty and complexity of the plant world. Whether in books or during my travels, plants became my lifelong companions, and my garden designs reflect this deep appreciation.

My journey to garden design started in earnest in 1997, when I launched my own design business. This decision followed years of study and personal growth. I had graduated from Emory University in Atlanta, Georgia, in 1986, with a major in psychology. Though my career path began in a completely different field, my passion for horticulture eventually guided me to the New York Botanical Garden, where I earned a certificate in commercial horticulture in 1998. That same year, I bought this house and began to experiment with the ideas I had learned.

One of the most significant moments in my development as a garden designer occurred in June 2000, when I had the opportunity to visit Hadspen House. This English garden, at the time managed by Nori and Sandra Pope, made a lasting impression on me. I had the privilege of spending a week there, participating in lectures and visiting other gardens, but it was the free time spent roaming Hadspen's borders that truly influenced my work. I was captivated by how the borders seamlessly melded from one color to another, with each plant combination more enchanting than the last. The use of color in the garden was exceptional, and I realized that creating these seamless transitions required

Opposite: A view down the 114-foot-long perennial garden. The *Fagus sylvatica* hedging has arms that break the garden into 14 individual beds. Some serve as circulation, some contain perennials and boxwoods arranged by color, some are left green to serve as a visual palate cleanser.

more than just planting ordinary species—it required precise attention to detail and a deep understanding of how colors could work together. This experience had a profound impact on my design philosophy, and when I returned home, I immediately added *Colour by Design*, the Popes' book, to my library.

Throughout my career, I have accumulated a library of more than 1,700 garden books—everything from rare antique volumes to the newest releases on plants and gardening. Each book holds a special place in my heart, as they represent the knowledge that continues to shape my understanding of plants and garden design. I've always been deeply inspired by the gardens I've visited around the world, but none have had a more lasting influence than those in England. The design principles I encountered at Hadspen House, combined with the beauty of the gardens I've explored, have shaped my vision and approach.

One of my most memorable gardening projects began in June 2010, when I received 176 bare root beech whips. Over the next few months, I prepared perennial beds, but the planting didn't begin until later that year. Hurricane Sandy, which struck in October 2012 and severely damaged this part of the garden, provided a sobering reminder of the challenges that gardeners face, especially when working with perennial plants. Despite the setbacks, I continued to refine my designs and focus on the beauty and resilience of plants.

My perennial border became a focal point, a place where I could experiment with the lessons learned from my travels, my study, and my work at Hadspen House. Each decision, from the choice of color to the selection of plants, was influenced by the desire to create something that would be both beautiful and enduring. It became clear that the way plants interact with each other, the colors they display, and the textures they offer, could transform a space and create a lasting impact.

This journey, from my first fascination with plants to my formal education and eventual career as a designer, has been shaped by the gardens I've encountered and the lessons I've learned along the way. As I continue to design and plant, I do so with the knowledge that every garden I create is not just a reflection of my vision but a testament to the plants that inspire me and the places that have influenced me. The perennial garden I've created is just one example of how the lessons of my travels, my studies, and my personal experiences come together to create something that I hope will stand the test of time, just like the gardens that have inspired me throughout my life.

Opposite: A composition of white *Orlaya grandiflora*, *Papaver* 'Princess Louise Victoria', and *Salvia* x *sylvestris* 'May Night'.

Overleaf: The simplicity of the *Fagus sylvatica* hedge's form masks the complexity and color hidden inside, among the double herbaceous borders.

Previous pages: This view into the perennial garden is how I mark the days and seasons, passing by every morning and evening. Ever-evolving, each day in the garden is truly a unique moment in time.

Left, above: The two most-used rooms of the house are aligned with a view to the perennial garden: the principal bedroom, above, and the living room with its bay window, below.

Left, below: A spray of *Knautia macedonica* beckons in front of custom gates leading to the perennial garden.

Opposite: *Orlaya grandiflora* planted in a steely white mass. It self-sows easily, making groupings achievable, but is not problematic or invasive.

Left: *Rosa* 'Madame Hardy' underplanted with *Alchemilla mollis*.

Right: Peering through the main gate reveals beds filled with peonies, lilies, and foxglove.

Left: A late-June view over and into the perennial garden.

Right: Blooms in full June glory. *Rosa* 'Bourbon Queen', above, and *Rosa* 'Charles de Mills', below.

Above, left: An emerging spire of wild white indigo (*Baptisia leucantha*).

Above, right: Waving stems of purple toadflax (*Linaria purpurea*).

Opposite: A grouping of lady's mantle (*Alchemilla mollis*).

Left: Peony 'Sarah Bernhardt' is paired with the deep pink of *Tanacetum coccineum*.

Right, above: A striped peony.

Right, below: *Paeonia* 'Festiva Maxima' with *Aquilegia* 'Black Barlow'.

Baptisia australis, above, and a yellow baptisia, opposite.

Above: *Lilium* beginning to unfurl, surrounded by golden Alexander (*Zizia aurea*).

Opposite: The vibrant umbels of *Zizia aurea*.

Overleaf: The perennial meadow in full-summer bloom, showing how the hedge delineates areas for specific compositions.

Left: The delicate seed heads of ornamental quaking grass (*Briza media*).

Right, above: Spending time in the garden each day is akin to meditation, allowing me to notice and appreciate every stage in a plant's life cycle, especially those that aren't normally celebrated.

Right, below: The sturdy stems of emerging lilies.

Above: *Papaver orientale* 'Raspberry Queen'.

Right: *Papaver orientale* 'Queen Alexandria'.

Above, clockwise from top left: *Iris* 'Easter Bonnet', *Iris* 'Dauntless', *Iris sibirica* 'Butter and Sugar', and *Iris* 'Amas'.

Opposite: *Iris sibirica* 'Caesar's Brother'.

Above: The long stems of *Knautia macedonica* help the blooms pop out and be noticed.

Right, above: The sculptural stems of *Phlomis tuberosa* 'Amazone'.

Right, below: The seed heads of ornamental grass *Briza media* are a study in geometry.

Opposite: Structure and form provided by the shaped hedging frame loose arrangements of perennials while keeping the overall mood formal.

Above: A honeybee visiting salvia blooms in the garden.

Overleaf: Sicilian honey garlic (*Nectaroscordum siculum*) blooms set off by the leaves of royal fern (*Osmunda regalis*).

Right: Rounded shrubs placed periodically throughout the perennial garden act as a visual foil to the more rectilinear "arms" of the hedge.

Overleaf: A simply shaped *Fagus sylvatica* hedge reads visually as sculpture, while acting practically as a divider between distinct areas of the garden.

FORM

When I think about form in a garden, I think of it as the skeleton of the landscape—the very framework upon which everything else is built. Form defines space, shapes the experience, and creates a visual language that communicates a garden's essence. It's more than just what's seen at first glance; it's the underpinning that supports and elevates all the other elements. Form is the starting point, the very building block of any thoughtful design. From it, the landscape unfolds, becoming a place that invites you to explore, to linger, and to connect with the natural world in meaningful ways.

Form, at its simplest, is created from lines. A single line might seem insignificant, but when combined with others, it becomes something powerful. A line can be straight or curving, sharp or gentle—each choice impacts the overall feel of the garden. These lines—whether used to edge a pathway, delineate a garden bed, or frame a view—serve as the foundation from which everything else emerges.

Once these lines come together, they create shapes, and when those shapes are arranged in patterns, form takes on more complexity. It becomes mass. And when discrete masses are combined thoughtfully, we achieve a composition—the final picture that we see and experience as a landscape. Annette Hoyt Flanders captured this beautifully when she said, "The plant material, architectural features, ornaments, and all materials used in creating landscape pictures are part of the design. They must all be chosen and combined so that the form, size, texture, and color of every item fits perfectly into and becomes an essential part of the harmonious whole."

In the garden, form isn't just about injecting visual appeal—it's about creating a space that has meaning and purpose. The forms that we choose to incorporate into a landscape help shape our experience. They guide the eye, influence movement, and create a rhythm that makes the space feel intentional. A straight-edged hedge might guide your attention toward a focal point. A sweeping curve might make a small space feel more expansive, and a bold, angular shape can add drama and interest.

The structure we create in a garden is rooted in form. It's the reason why a garden feels cohesive, purposeful, and inviting. I often say that underlying forms are the "bones" of the landscape. While perennials, annuals, and flowers certainly add beauty and vibrancy, it's the hardscape—walls, pathways, terraces—and the larger trees and shrubs that form the structural foundation. These elements provide crucial support and definition.

One of the most important aspects of creating structure is division. A garden that is divided into smaller spaces with unique elements or themes always feels larger and more inviting than one that is left open and exposed. Small, intimate spaces encourage exploration. You're drawn to them, pulled in to discover what's just around the corner. In a larger, undivided landscape, the eye can take in the entire space in a glance, and that instant impression leaves no room for curiosity. It's too quick, too easy to grasp.

By thoughtfully dividing the space and layering different forms—hedges, trees, walls, and paths—a garden becomes dynamic. Layering creates depth, allowing light and shadow to play off one another, creating contrast and interest. Transitions between spaces, from one form to another, encourage the visitor to move through the landscape at a slower pace. Time feels as though it slows when we step into a space that is divided, defined.

In the climates where I work, winter plays an especially important role in the garden. The landscape undergoes a dramatic transformation during the colder months, with many plants fading and shedding their leaves, leaving behind only the bare bones of the design. And it is during this time that the foundational forms—evergreen hedges, walls, and other structural elements—truly come into their own.

Evergreens like boxwood and yew are the workhorses of the winter garden. They provide a much-needed sense of structure and color when the rest of the landscape is dormant. The rich green of a carefully shaped hedge, its form standing strong against the backdrop of a gray sky and bare branches,

Opposite: *Taxus baccata* 'Hicksii' domes and a *Ligustrum vulgare* hedge sheared into tight forms.

brings a sense of life and continuity to the garden during the bleak months. These hedges not only define space but also provide shelter for wildlife, offering a place of refuge against the harsh winter winds.

When designing for winter, the emphasis on form becomes even more critical. Without the flowers and foliage that provide seasonal interest, the garden relies on its structural elements to provide beauty and definition. A mature hedge, shaped and maintained over the years, becomes a statement piece in itself. It's more than just a boundary—it's an essential part of the landscape, one that enhances the garden's form year round.

These hedges, along with other foundational elements, become anchors in the garden, holding the space together and providing a sense of permanence. The layering of evergreens, along with deciduous trees and shrubs that contribute form even in winter, ensures that the garden remains visually interesting even when the flowers have faded.

Another aspect of form that I always consider when designing is the relationship between the interior of a home and the garden outside. A garden is not a separate entity from the house; it's an extension of it. The forms we choose for the garden should harmonize with the architecture of the house, enhancing the experience of both.

From inside the home, the view of the garden should be framed, composed, and intentional. The lines of the garden should draw the eye outward, creating a sense of connection between the two spaces. Windows, doors, and openings are like picture frames for the landscape outside. Just as a piece of art in a frame draws your attention, the garden outside should capture your gaze and invite you to experience its beauty. The forms in the garden should feel as though they belong to the house, as though they were always meant to be a part of the view.

Form is the backbone of garden design. It provides the structure, defines the space, and gives the garden its sense of purpose. Whether in the lush green of summer or the stark quiet of winter, form holds the landscape together, creating a space that feels intentional and harmonious. From the careful placement of hedges to the strategic use of mass and pattern, form is the foundation on which all else is built. It is the key to crafting a landscape that invites exploration, sparks curiosity, and offers beauty—no matter the season.

Opposite: *Buxus sempervirens* provides green even in deepest winter, while *Fagus sylvatica* contributes color as well as form.

Overleaf: Six large squares of *Buxus sempervirens*, with domed centers for visual interest.

Above and opposite: Low *Buxus sempervirens* hedges surround the front terrace; pachysandra is used as a groundcover on the far perimeter. Ultimately the pachysandra has been replaced with no-mow fescue, which tolerates the southern exposure much better.

CHAPTER THREE

THE MEADOW

The meadow is one of the quieter corners of the property, though it's always teeming with life. It stretches out next to the vegetable garden and just beyond the greenhouse, a soft patch of wildness that contrasts with the more cultivated spaces—including the manicured lawns and perfectly planned garden beds. It's an untamed beauty that works in harmony with everything else, providing texture and rhythm to the landscape.

One of the first plants to make its presence known in the meadow is *Penstemon digitalis*, a tall, graceful flower that blooms in soft spikes of white and pale purple. Their spires rise above the grasses, drawing the eye, and in the early mornings, when the dew still clings to the petals, they seem almost otherworldly, like delicate, architectural porcelain towers scattered throughout an otherwise uncultivated expanse. I love the quietness of those first blooms each year—they promise that the meadow, though wild and untended, will soon burst into a chorus of color and life.

There's something magical about watching the meadow evolve through the seasons. Early in the year, it's full of green shoots, the plants still reaching for the sky. As the warmth of summer settles in, it becomes a riot of wildflowers, grasses, and herbs. One of my favorite plants here is milkweed, which grows in dense clusters. It's a plant that serves more than one purpose—its most important perhaps as a home to monarch butterflies. I'll often see the butterflies drifting lazily through the air, their orange wings glowing like a flame against the backdrop of green. The milkweed is their sanctuary, where they can lay their eggs and where the hatching caterpillars feed. It's an honor to know that the meadow serves as part of their migratory journey, offering a brief but important stop along the way.

Opposite: *Penstemon digitalis*, *Asclepias incarnata*, and grasses form a meadow.

In the evenings, as the sun dips behind the hills, the meadow takes on a completely different character. Crickets begin their symphony, their rhythmic chirps filling the air. And if you're lucky enough to be outside just as night falls, the fireflies emerge, their tiny lanterns flickering in the dusk. It's a sight to behold—tiny, glowing specks dancing through the grasses, like stars fallen to earth, alive with movement. I can stand there for hours, watching them, marveling at the way they light up the darkness in such a gentle, fleeting way.

The meadow is more than just a visual pleasure; it's a habitat. The grasses and wildflowers are home to a whole host of small creatures and insects. Bees, of course, love it here. Though they're mostly drawn to the vegetable garden and the flowers in the greenhouse, they spend time in the meadow too, drifting from one flower to the next. I've even seen rabbits skittering between the tall grasses, the occasional deer passing through in the early-morning hours when the air is still cool. If you sit still long enough, you might spot a family of field mice darting from one patch of cover to another. It's a living, breathing ecosystem, each part contributing to the whole.

What I love most about the meadow is that it doesn't demand constant care. Unlike the rest of the garden, where I'm always tending to the plants, pruning, watering, and weeding, the meadow requires nothing but a little patience. It takes weekly mowing out of the equation—something I never minded, but something that always felt like another item on the to-do list. Instead, the meadow takes care of itself, growing and changing with the seasons, offering different views at every turn.

In the spring, it's a lush green, dotted with the first wildflowers. In summer, the grasses grow tall, swaying with the breeze, and the flowers bloom in a riot of colors. Come fall, the meadow softens, the colors of the plants fading into browns, yellows, and reds as they prepare for winter's rest. In winter, it's still, quiet, a place of retreat for the animals that remain. The texture of the meadow changes with the seasons, always offering something new to look at, to appreciate, and to admire.

There's also something about the way it's positioned next to the beehives that makes it even more special. The meadow provides a buffer, a space where the bees can fly freely without being disturbed by human activity. It's a quiet place for them to forage, a place where they can go about their work uninterrupted. I think of the meadow as a sort of sanctuary for the bees, a place where they can rest and gather nectar in peace. And in return, the bees pollinate the wildflowers, the grasses, the herbs, creating a reciprocal relationship that benefits everyone.

I've always felt a deep connection to the meadow. It's a place that doesn't require much from me, yet offers so much in return. It teaches me about the cycles of nature—how things grow, bloom, and fade in their own time. It's a reminder that, sometimes, less is more. We don't always need to control every detail. Sometimes, if we let go and allow nature to take its course, it will provide beauty in ways we never expected.

The meadow is its own world; it operates at a different rhythm than the rest of the farm, but one that is no less important. It's a place of peace and quiet, of hidden life and unexpected moments of wonder. And I know that no matter how much the rest of the farm changes, the meadow will remain—a constant, evolving beauty in the heart of it all.

Previous pages: The meadow in early summer, with the *Penstemon digitalis* in bloom.

Left, above: *Asclepias* starting in the meadow.

Left, below: Milkweed pods split open in late summer so the wind can disperse its seeds.

Baby wild turkeys occasionally parade through the meadow.

A view across the meadow, looking toward the vegetable garden.

Looking across the meadow
toward the greenhouse garden.

The meadow is composed mostly of grasses; observing what pollinators and animals visit in every phase—as they grow, bloom, and fade into strawlike colors in fall is a joy.

Above: If we look carefully, we'll see that each and every blade of grass is its own sculpture.

Opposite: Simple oxeye daisies (*Leucanthemum vulgare*) fit well as members of the meadow.

Overleaf: Late in the season is when the wild carrot (*Daucus carota*) comes into its own in the meadow.

UMBELS

I've always been drawn to plants with a certain air of grace—plants that stand tall but don't demand attention, those that lend themselves to a quieter kind of beauty. The Apiaceae family, or umbellifers, embodies this perfectly. They have a subtlety and elegance that's not just visually appealing but that also contributes significantly to the texture and movement in the garden. These plants give the garden a sense of rhythm, with their umbrella-shaped flower heads and finely cut foliage, offering a beautiful contrast to the more traditional, bushy flowers we often think of in the garden.

In my perennial gardens, umbellifers have become indispensable. Whether it's the delicate, lacelike appearance of Queen Anne's lace or the bold, striking presence of *Angelica gigas*, this family of plants brings a balance of structure and softness, height, and delicacy. These plants stand as pillars in the garden while still offering lightness, as if floating above everything else.

Let's start with *Daucus carota*, or Queen Anne's lace. I've always admired how this plant seems to effortlessly fill space without taking over. Its delicate, lacy white blooms remind me of old-fashioned gardens—romantic, understated, and nostalgic. What I love about Queen Anne's lace is how it acts as a transitional plant, effortlessly moving between the boldness of perennial flowers and the more delicate and wild edges of a meadow.

Its ability to draw the eye with its simple yet exquisite flowerheads is unparalleled. It's a wonderful addition to a naturalistic garden or one where I want to mix textures and forms. I often place it beside plants with a more rigid structure, such as boxwoods or ornamental grasses. The fine, lacelike flowers soften the hard lines, creating a harmonious blend of textures and forms.

Queen Anne's lace is also excellent at attracting pollinators, particularly beneficial insects like bees and butterflies. This not only benefits the overall health of the garden but adds a layer of motion and life that can be magical, especially when the wind rustles through its feathery flowers.

Next on my list is *Foeniculum vulgare* 'Purpureum', or bronze fennel. The deep burgundy color of its feathery foliage contrasts beautifully with the golden umbels of flowers that appear later in the season. I love how bronze fennel adds an air of sophistication and drama to the garden. The rich color of the leaves grounds the planting, while the delicate, airy flowers add a light touch.

The feathery texture of the bronze fennel's foliage is one of its standout features. It contrasts beautifully with the larger leaves of plants like *Helenium* or *Echinacea*, providing a wonderful balance. Plus, its height and airy quality make it a great plant for the back of a bed or as a statement piece near a path or garden entrance. And, like other umbellifers, it attracts beneficial insects, making it a great addition for encouraging a healthy ecosystem.

Angelica gigas is another member of the umbellifer family that I can't resist. With its deep purple stems and large, dramatic umbels of pinkish flowers, it adds a sense of grandeur to any garden. It stands tall and proud, often reaching heights of five feet or more, and its large leaves create a sense of substance in the garden.

I love the architectural quality it brings to the landscape. Placing it near lower-growing perennials helps draw the eye upward, creating vertical interest and offering a lovely contrast to the more rounded or compact plants. Its size and bold color make it an ideal centerpiece for a garden that's seeking a more dramatic look, and it pairs well with the softer forms of plants like *Ammi majus* or *Anthriscus sylvestris*.

Ammi majus is another umbellifer that I often turn to for its delicate, lacelike flowers. Known as false Queen Anne's lace, *Ammi majus*, has a more refined, almost ethereal appearance. The white flowers seem to shimmer in the garden, creating a sense of lightness and transparency. I find this plant works wonders when I want to soften the edges of a garden or introduce a more fluid quality.

Ammi majus is excellent for filling in gaps and creating airy layers of texture. It pairs beautifully with darker-leaved plants

Opposite: Exuberant and cheerful *Angelica archangelica*.

such as *Ligularia* or *Hellebore*, where its pale flowers contrast strikingly with the deep greens and purples of the foliage. I also love using it as a filler between more solid plants, where it can create an open, almost magical quality.

The *Angelica* genus offers some of the most striking plants in the umbellifer family. *Angelica archangelica*, with its large, greenish-yellow umbels and broad, deeply cut leaves, is a plant that feels almost ancient, like something you might find in a medieval herb garden. Its striking, statuesque form adds instant drama to any garden, particularly when placed against a backdrop of more neutral greenery or in a shaded area where it can thrive.

Angelica pachycarpa has a more compact and rounded form but still carries that distinctive *Angelica* charm. Its dense, globe-like flowers stand out against the dark green foliage, creating a sense of fullness that's both elegant and practical. I tend to use it as an anchor plant in a bed, giving structure while not overpowering the surrounding plants.

Then there's *Ligusticum scoticum*, or Scottish lovage. This plant is a quieter presence in the garden but no less beautiful. The finely divided foliage and small, creamy-white flowers create a subtle texture that's perfect for softening the transitions between other plants. It doesn't compete for attention but instead enhances the overall aesthetic of the garden. I love how it adds depth and layering, especially when planted with other, more colorful flowers.

Minoa lace (*Orlaya grandiflora*) is another fascinating member of the umbellifer family. The white, lacy flowers are just as delicate as *Ammi majus*, but with a slightly more refined and airy presence. It's perfect for planting in a perennial garden, where it can fill in the gaps between other flowers while still creating an elegant, cohesive look. An added benefit is that it self-seeds reliably. Its soft, fernlike foliage also provides great texture, particularly when paired with plants that have broader or waxy leaves. *Anthriscus sylvestris* 'Ravenswing'—with its dark, almost black leaves—provides a striking contrast to lighter-colored plants. The combination of the dark foliage and the fine, lace-like umbels of white flowers gives the garden a gothic quality, perfect for adding depth and drama. It's a plant that stands out without screaming for attention, a quiet but bold addition.

Pimpinella is another umbellifer that often catches my eye for its delicate beauty. Its small, dainty flowers form airy, rounded umbels that add texture and lightness to a planting scheme. I use *Pimpinella* to fill in the gaps between more dominant plants, its soft flowers and fine leaves acting as a perfect contrast to more solid forms.

Finally, there's *Peucedanum verticillare*, a towering plant with a striking presence. It's one of those plants that commands attention but in the most understated way. The feathery foliage and large, rounded flower heads add height without bulk. It's a wonderful plant to use at the back of a border, where its delicate flowers can offer a stunning visual effect, especially when paired with other bold plants like *Phlomis*.

I've come to rely on the *Apiaceae* family plants in my garden not just for their beauty but for their ability to add structure, texture, and movement to the landscape. Whether it's the towering presence of *Angelica gigas*, the fine lace of *Ammi majus*, or the dark elegance of *Anthriscus sylvestris* 'Ravenswing', each plant in the family brings something unique to the table. They're the quiet, elegant contributors to the perennial garden, offering both harmony and contrast in the landscape.

The beauty of the umbellifers lies in their versatility. They can be bold or subtle, but always add an element of grace that transforms the garden into something dynamic, textured, and full of life. For me, these plants are the backbone of a garden that's meant to be as much about movement, light, and structure as it is about beauty. The umbellifers teach me that simplicity can hold great power and that the quiet plants often carry the most profound impact.

Opposite: *Orlaya grandiflora* planted en masse.

Overleaf: I always try to remind myself to pause and take a close look even at plants that are familiar; even observing the petals of these *Orlaya grandiflora* flowers at different stages of maturity is a deeply gratifying pursuit.

Pages 116–17: A calm swath of lawn accentuates the burst of texture that characterizes the late-summer meadow, particularly the flowers of *Daucus carota*, the white blooms scattered throughout.

CHAPTER FOUR

THE GREENHOUSE

The idea of having a greenhouse grew within me for many years before I acted on it, from a simple seed of inspiration into something that now exists as a place of refuge, beauty, and peace. My journey toward building the greenhouse began in 1999, when I first read the works of Beverly Nichols. His books, particularly *Down the Garden Path*, had a profound impact on me. It was in these pages that I found two short paragraphs that resonated deeply, and still echo in my mind today. Nichols wrote about the sanctuary of a greenhouse, a space where one could escape the wildness of the outside world and experience the peace and security only it can offer.

To Nichols, the greenhouse was a haven, a space protected from the elements outside. He described the joy of stepping into a greenhouse during a fierce storm, hearing the rain slashing against the roof, feeling the wind howl beyond the walls, yet knowing that inside, all was calm. "To go to the greenhouse when the weather is wild, to close the door, to stand and listen to the wind outside, to the rain that slashes the frail roof...to savour to the full the strange and almost uncanny peace which this frail tenement creates," he wrote. These words captured my imagination and inspired me to eventually add my own greenhouse.

The concept of installing a greenhouse became more tangible over the years, but it wasn't until June 6, 2007, that I took the first step toward making it a reality. That day, I received a brochure and letter from Alitex, a company based in England that specializes in greenhouses. I had been dreaming of one for years, but now, I had the information I needed to move forward. However, it wasn't until October 2015, eight years later, that construction finally began. By then, I had already spent years collecting plants from my various travels, including from the Caribbean, and I could already envision how they would look in a space where I could nurture and display them all.

Opposite: The approach to the greenhouse features a *Carpinus betulus* hedge and a custom gate.

In 2016, the greenhouse structure arrived, perfectly timed with my birthday, and by May of that year, it was up and running. My agapanthus, which had been living in the garage, were the first to move into the new space, and they have flourished ever since. The greenhouse quickly became more than just a place to house plants; it became a space of sensory experience—a place of color, light, and atmosphere. Nichols described the magic of a greenhouse with such clarity that I felt like I had experienced it myself, long before I ever stepped foot in one. The feeling of standing in that peaceful, fragrant space, protected even as I listened to the rain as it beat against the glass roof, was something I had longed for, and it was finally within my reach.

The greenhouse has since become a sanctuary for me, a place where I can escape the hustle and bustle of daily life and immerse myself in the simple joy of nurturing plants. The smell of damp soil, the sight of lush greenery, and the sound of rain tapping against the glass all create an atmosphere that transports me to a different world—a world that feels as though it exists outside of time. Much like Nichols, I relish the peace that the greenhouse offers, especially when the weather outside is wild. There's a strange security in knowing that, inside, nothing can harm the plants or me.

I've also come to appreciate the joy of plant collecting in this space. It's not just about the plants themselves, but about the memories they carry. Many of the plants I've gathered in my travels now call the greenhouse home, and each one reminds me of a different place and experience. The greenhouse has allowed me to curate a collection of plants from around the world, all thriving in their own little corner of this sanctuary.

Today, I realize that the greenhouse is more than just a physical structure; it's a reflection of my own journey and the values that I hold dear. It's a place where I can reconnect with nature, with the serenity that comes from nurturing life, and with the joy of creating something beautiful. And just as Nichols so eloquently described, it is in the greenhouse that I find a deep, almost uncanny peace—a peace that has become one of the truest joys life has given me.

Previous pages: I collect pelargoniums and tropical plants, both of which are happy in the greenhouse even in Connecticut winters.

Opposite, above: Variegated kumquats are a citrusy addition to the collection of tender plants housed here.

Opposite, below: Rose-scented pelargoniums release their fragrance when the leaves are brushed or bumped.

Left: A side view through the Alitex greenhouse, which features doors on opposite sides, greatly improving access.

Right, above: Many of the plants in the greenhouse are specimens I encountered in my travels, including *Opuntia ficus-indica*.

Right, below: *Sedum nussbaumerianum*, remarkable for its coppery color when grown in full sun, is native to Mexico and often used as a groundcover in warmer climates.

Left, above: *Kalanchoe daigremontiana*, commonly known as "mother of thousands," is native to Madagascar.

Left, below: *Euphorbia flanaganii*, which has the colorful common name of "Medusa's head plant."

Above: Specimen trees in Versailles-style planters painted to compliment the greenhouse's exterior and cold frames flank one entrance.

Overleaf: A close-up view of *Cosmos atrosanguineus* and *Phlebodium aureum* is a study in microcosmic form.

Left and overleaf: A table and chairs from Munder Skiles make it possible to host drinks or lunch in the greenhouse, though often as not the chairs host pots full of plants.

COLOR

There's one color in the garden that always seems to elevate everything else around it, a color that brings depth and sophistication to the landscape. It's a rich, almost regal shade of burgundy, and I have learned over the years that it does more than just catch the eye—it has the remarkable ability to make everything around it look better. When I think of plants that are burgundy, I think first of *Knautia macedonica*, one of my absolute favorites for its deep, velvety blooms that never fail to command attention.

Burgundy isn't a color I would describe as brash or loud. It doesn't shout or demand attention in the same way a brilliant red might. Instead, it speaks with quiet authority, adding a sense of gravitas to any space it inhabits. And in the garden, where color and texture play off each other, burgundy is the perfect counterpoint to the lighter tones of greens and blues. It's the kind of color that simply makes everything around it suddenly feel more vibrant, more cohesive. It grounds the garden while still adding that touch of drama that keeps things interesting.

I first fell for *Knautia macedonica* years ago, when I saw it in a friend's garden. The flowers are dusky, almost like an aged wine, but with a paradoxically delicate, almost whimsical shape. They look as if a painter must have dreamed them up, a soft contrast of color and form. The blooms rise from sturdy stems held high above the surrounding foliage, and they're always a welcome sight. They don't try to dominate the garden, but they enhance everything around them—playing beautifully with other plants. They would fit well in every corner of the landscape. I've planted them in several spots over the years, always strategically placed where I want to add a touch of depth.

What I love most about *Knautia* is how it contrasts so wonderfully with blues and greens, particularly the vibrant blue of *Salvia* or the cool tones of *Nepeta* and *Echinops*. The burgundy shades of *Knautia* have a way of acting as a foil to the cooler tones, making them appear even brighter, more intense. It's a marriage of colors that feels effortless, natural, yet is incredibly striking.

Burgundy isn't just confined to flowers, though. I've planted *Acer platanoides* 'Crimson King', a dark-leaved maple that offers such a rich backdrop in the garden. The leaves, with their deep, reddish-purple hue, lend a stately air to any area they occupy. They don't just stand out—they enrich the whole garden, offering a backdrop that makes lighter greens and yellows pop. This tree has a way of drawing the eye, pulling you in with its color and elegance, but it doesn't overwhelm. It becomes part of the garden's subtle symphony, creating a sense of balance and calm.

Then there's *Cotinus coggygria* 'Royal Purple', or the royal purple smoke bush, another favorite of mine. The smoky purple leaves, tinged with burgundy, have a certain ethereal quality. When the sun hits them just right, the backlit leaves seem to glow. In summer, it stands tall and proud, its wispy, smokelike plumes adding texture to the landscape. In autumn, it's the burgundy tones of the leaves that take center stage, a glorious show that fills the garden with deep, glowing color before the leaves fall to the ground.

But it's *Knautia macedonica* that always feels like the perfect anchor for all these other burgundy beauties. Its subtle, almost architectural shape contrasts nicely with the rounded blooms of *Cosmos atrosanguineus*, another dark burgundy flower I hold dear. Its rich, chocolatey color of pairs perfectly with *Knautia*, both offering a deep contrast to the lighter greens of foliage or the soft blues of neighboring plants. Together, they create a visual rhythm in the garden—a balance between softness and structure, lightness and weight.

Burgundy has this magical way of transforming a garden, creating depth and interest without being overpowering. It's the color of refinement, of elegance, and yet, when it's placed among the right companions, it's not at all fussy or pretentious. It's a color that enhances, elevates, and enriches everything it touches.

In a way, burgundy is the quiet heart of the garden. It's the color you don't always notice at first, but once you see it, it's impossible to forget. And when it's paired with the delicate blooms of *Knautia*, or the soft glow of a crimson-leaved tree, it becomes something more than just a color. It's an experience, one that adds a sense of timelessness and sophistication to the landscape, making everything around it feel more connected, more intentional, and infinitely more beautiful.

Opposite: The blooms of *Knautia macedonica* are one of nature's truest magentas.

Previous pages: One of two mature *Acer platanoides* 'Crimson King' on the property, which feature maroon leaves all growing season.

Opposite, top: *Cotinus coggygria* 'Royal Purple' in bloom, soon to display the billowy puffs that give the plant its nickname of "smokebush."

Opposite, bottom left: While the smokebush's flowers often steal the show, its bluish-green leaves with prominent veining deserve a glance, too.

Opposite, bottom right: *Penstemon digitalis* 'Husker Red' has leaves that present as maroon early in the season and mature to a dark green late in the season.

Right: *Rosa glauca* is a cold-hardy shrub rose that features foliage in a blend of plum and gray-green and reddish canes, in addition of course to its delicate pink flowers.

Previous pages: The maroon foliage of the towering *Acer platanoides* adds depth and contrast to the overall garden.

The bushy white blooms of *Paeonia* 'Festiva Maxima' make the flowers of *Aquilegia* 'Black Barlow' appear particularly deep in contrast.

CHAPTER FIVE

THE TROUGH GARDEN

Antiques have a way of weaving themselves into a garden, infusing it with character and a sense of history that feels both grounding and timeless. In my own garden, these pieces—some of them aged gracefully, others repurposed—do much to personalize the space. They're not just ornaments or relics; they're vessels of memory and meaning, anchoring the garden in a way that no new object can replicate. Every antique I've placed has a story, and each one adds depth to the narrative of the garden itself.

One of my favorite spots in the garden is the area off the covered porch. Here, a limestone trough has been transformed into a water feature. The trough's rough, weathered exterior contrasts beautifully with the lush greenery that surrounds it, but it's the sound of the water flowing over the stone that truly makes this spot magical. It's creates a serene moment in the garden when the outside world melts away and the gentle trickling of water creates a sense of calm. From both the family room and the porch, you can hear it, and it's become a beloved background soundtrack to many quiet evenings spent at home. In the drier months, the trough serves another purpose—it becomes a watering hole for the local birds. They perch on the rim, delicate and unaware of the world around them, sipping the cool water. I've found that the water feature, though a simple enough structure, provides the opportunity for meaningful connections to the creatures that visit.

By night, it transforms. I've installed a soft internal light within the trough, which casts a shimmering glow onto the large oak tree that stands above. The glow, reflected off the water, creates a hauntingly beautiful play of light and shadow. It keeps the garden feeling alive, even after the sun has gone down. The oak, an imposing figure during the day, becomes a graceful silhouette in the dark, its branches swaying gently in the breeze. There's something about the interplay of light and shadow that feels like a secret only the night can reveal.

Opposite: This antique limestone trough is set in a gravel bed surrounded by bluestone turned on edge. I repurposed it as a fountain to add a subtle burbling and lit it to add interest to this corner of the garden in the evenings.

Beyond the water feature, scattered throughout the garden, are other antiques that hold their own special place. Two hexagonal stone fragments from a forgotten monument now serve as stools on the covered porch. When I first found them, I wasn't sure what they were meant to be, but their proportions were perfect, and they seemed to invite seating. With time, they've settled into the garden as if they've always belonged there, their edges softened by the years, the weight of history in their presence.

Two lead doves with fanned tails, perched high on a stone pedestal, overlook the pool garden. I found them at an antique market years ago, weathered and faded from time, but they have a certain grace about them that makes them feel at home. The doves face each other. There's something peaceful in their stance, like two sentinels keeping watch over the space. They've come to symbolize a quiet serenity in the garden—a sense of balance and harmony that I hope visitors feel when they walk by them.

Outside the perennial garden, matching plinths stand tall, adorned with intricate carvings of holly leaves. I was thrilled when I came across these—they're such a perfect embodiment of the seasons, and their level of craftsmanship is rarely found in today's world of mass production. Atop these plinths, I placed two carved-stone planters, which are filled with agaves in the warmer months. The agaves' spiky, architectural forms contrast with the softness of the holly carvings below them, and together they create a striking, almost sculptural pairing. There's something about the juxtaposition of the organic and the crafted that makes these pieces so interesting, and in the changing seasons, they offer a reminder of the beauty of both permanence and transformation.

Then, there's the sundial at the center of the vegetable garden. It features a sunflower motif, a symbol of the sun's warmth and the seasons' cyclical nature. I've always loved the idea of a sundial; it's a beautiful reminder that time passes not only with the ticking of a clock but with the slow, natural rhythm of the earth. The sunflower, with its wide, open face, seems to capture the essence of summer in a way that no other symbol can. In the morning, the sunlight catches the sundial just right, casting long shadows that move throughout the day. It's another small but significant element that adds depth to the garden—something both practical and poetic.

Each of these antiques, in their own way, tells a story. Some are reminders of my travels and the places I've visited, while others are echoes of forgotten eras, repurposed and reimagined in the context of this garden. The beauty of garden antiques lies in their ability to connect the past with the present, creating a sense of continuity and layering within the garden. They ground the space, making it feel not just like a collection of plants and features, but like a living history.

When I walk through the garden, I'm reminded of how these objects carry the weight of time with them. They are a celebration of craftsmanship, of attention to detail, and of a love for beauty that transcends generations. And though the plants may change with the seasons, the antiques remain constant, creating a timeless backdrop for the ever-evolving garden. In many ways, they make the garden feel more personal—each piece a reflection of my tastes, my travels, and the moments that have shaped my life.

Antiques, with their weathered surfaces and storied pasts, bring a depth to the garden that can't be achieved with new things. They offer a sense of place, a feeling of rootedness, and a quiet invitation to reflect on the beauty of both the past and the present. And as the years go by, these pieces will continue to tell their stories, grounding the garden in the richness of history even while it grows and changes with each passing season.

Opposite: This area of the garden is bordered by European beech (*Fagus sylvatica*) hedging on three sides and given a backdrop of six tiered, espaliered linden trees (*Tilia* sp.).

A full view of the trough garden, which is given a strong-but-lush border to define it as a separate and unique area within the larger property.

Left and opposite: A matching pair of plinth bases purchased in England are set on four-inch-thick bluestone to keep them raised above the ground in winter. Each year, once danger of frost has passed, I plant the urns with *Agave americana*.

Opposite: An antique sundial sits in the middle of the vegetable garden; a wooden tuteur patiently waits to support climbing plants later in the season.

Above: An antique copper pot is filled with still water to support wildlife and pollinators.

Opposite: The covered porch offers respite and a place to entertain.

Right, above: Antique stone plinths fitted with custom cushions create extra seating.

Right, below: A view to the covered porch through two of the matching custom gates that dot the property.

Following pages: A kissing bench of English oak by Gaze Burvill.

Pages 157–58: The antique trough sits on axis with the covered porch as well as on axis with the gamecock house.

CIRCULATION

There's something deeply satisfying about the moment when a house and garden finally come together, when the inside and the outside seem to communicate seamlessly, almost as if they were always meant to be one. It's a connection that doesn't happen by accident but through careful design—an intentional flow allows you to experience both spaces in a harmonious way. The question is: how best to achieve this connection? How do you create a sense of unity between the interior spaces and the outdoor surroundings so both feel like extensions of one another, not separate entities?

There are two paths to consider: one is visual, the other physical. Both are essential, and together, they form the foundation of a landscape that doesn't just surround the home but complements and enhances it.

Let's start with the visual path. This is all about how the house and garden relate when viewed from inside. The goal here is to create moments of intrigue that invite you to look outside, that draw your attention to a particular focal point in the garden. Every room in a house should have a planned view—a scene that pleases the eye. It's much better to gaze out onto a thoughtfully designed garden than to be constantly distracted by something less pleasant on a neighboring property, for example. This isn't just a matter of aesthetics; it's about creating a sense of calm and focus, offering a moment of respite each time you look out the window.

One way to establish visual connection is through by creating a long axial perspective. Imagine standing in a room, looking out through a set of French doors, your gaze guided by a pathway that stretches beyond the threshold. This path can be designed to lead the eye straight toward a central feature, perhaps a beautifully placed garden ornament, a fountain, or a large specimen tree. The act of following this line—starting from the interior of the house and flowing outward into the garden—creates a sense of purpose. The design that makes the viewer feel as if they are intended to be led somewhere. At night, the same pathway could be dramatically illuminated, turning that garden feature into a glowing focal point, instantly drawing attention and creating interest, even in the dark. Visual links like these make the outside world feel more accessible, more connected to the inside of the home, and they imbue the entire space with a sense of thoughtfulness. We can sense when someone *conceived* a layout. There is intention behind every line, every curve. The details, the careful consideration of how light falls on the path, the placement of the ornament, are what make a garden special.

But there's another layer to this connection, one that is more experiential. The physical ties that link the house and the garden are just as important, perhaps even more so. These are the moments you feel as you move through the garden—the tactile experience of walking down a path, passing through an allée of trees or shrubs, or entering a garden room enclosed by hedges. It's about creating a journey, one that unfolds as you move through the space, offering you a new perspective with every step.

A great garden isn't static, it's dynamic. Nature constantly changes with the seasons, evolving over time, and a good garden enhances our awareness of these shifts. The act of walking through it allows you to experience these changes firsthand. The sound of leaves rustling in the wind, the trickle of a nearby stream, the scent of a fragrant shrub as you pass by—these are the details that enhance the sensory experience of being in the garden. They add richness to the space, inviting you to pause, to breathe, to fully immerse yourself in the moment.

Enclosed spaces in the garden, such as hedged garden rooms, are particularly effective at creating this sense of discovery. These spaces paradoxically feel larger than they are; a sequestered space can offer an almost theatrical experience, and by sharpening your senses to what's right in front of you, the richness of the whole experience is enhanced. You might walk through a narrow opening only to be greeted by a dramatic shift in the landscape—an intimate courtyard, a quiet sitting area, or a sculpture that serves as a focal point.

Opposite: The *Buxus sempervirens* squares sit on axis with the pool garden's entry.

Garden rooms invite exploration and, in doing so, create a deeper connection between the house and its surroundings. A house set in a well-conceived garden feels like a whole, not two separate parts.

The physical ties that connect the garden back to the house are equally important. It's crucial that the garden feels like an extension of the living space, not something separate or distant. Pathways should lead back to the house, guiding you effortlessly between the interior and the garden. Outdoor entertaining spaces, such as a dining area or a sitting nook, should be placed just off the house, creating a fluid transition from the indoors to the outdoors. A framed view of the house from the garden, perhaps through a trellis or an archway, reinforces this connection and reminds you that the two spaces are intrinsically linked.

In the end, circulation—whether it's visual or physical—is all about the relationship between the house and garden. It's about making sure that neither exists in isolation. The way the garden unfolds before you, the way the light changes as you walk through it, and the way the house and garden interact visually—these elements together create a space that feels both purposeful and serene. A garden that is linked seamlessly to the house doesn't just enhance the property—it becomes an integral part of it.

Opposite: The *Buxus sempervirens* square hedges also align with the side entrance to the perennial garden.

Overleaf: The double gates in the greenhouse garden align with the trough garden and gamecock house.

CHAPTER SIX

THE PRODUCTIVE GARDEN

The vegetable garden, a sprawling patch of land measuring 110 feet long by 75 feet wide, is my sanctuary. It's divided into twenty-two beds, each 3 feet wide, some long and others shorter, but each one crafted to suit the crops I want to grow. The beds have a rhythm to them—a flow that, over time, has become familiar, like the beat of a well-loved song. The beds sit on a lawn that I've carefully tended, surrounded by hedges and gates, creating a room of its own in the midst of the larger farm.

I vividly remember the first moment I knew how I would shape this space. It was March 9, 2011, and I was wandering the aisles of a wholesale nursery on Long Island, scouting materials for future projects. As I perused, my gaze caught a row of *Taxus* x *media* 'Hicksii,' large, dark green shrubs standing five feet tall, their dense foliage almost hypnotic. A vision of those hedges circling a vegetable garden instantly appeared in my mind. The idea of a new, more defined space where vegetables and flowers could thrive, enclosed and protected, felt right. It was an instinctive decision, one I didn't need to think too much about. I knew, without a doubt, that I had to have them. The nursery had just enough plants for me to create the new hedge that would define the vegetable garden.

By March 23, the yews had been delivered to my driveway. And so began the transformation. A trench was dug around the garden to accommodate the new hedging, which would become the boundary of a new room on the farm. The work was vigorous but satisfying. By March 31, the trenching had progressed well, and by April 25, just in time for spring, the interior beds were finally cut in. The vegetable garden had been reborn, its layout crisp and clean, ready to be filled with life.

Opposite: Gooseberries in the vegetable garden.

Part of the history of this farm has to do with the soil. Once, it was entirely self-sufficient, with poultry, livestock, and gardens that fed the household and gave it back nutrients. Homemade butter was churned in the kitchen, and fresh produce was grown in abundance. I had a vision to revive the horticultural side of the property. The vegetable garden became the heart of that revival.

The new taxus hedging would enclose not just vegetables but also the flowers, herbs, and fruits that now fill the garden. Along with the tomatoes, asparagus, lettuce, and other hearty vegetables, there's a deep patch of fragrant herbs tucked around an antique sundial that sits proudly at the center. The sundial is more than a marker of time—it's a symbol of the patience required to tend everything that grows here. Thyme, basil, rosemary, and parsley spill out from their beds, their fragrances mingling with the soil and air, ready to be plucked for the kitchen.

But it's not just about the vegetables. Dahlias, in every shade of pink, red, orange, and white, bloom tirelessly through the growing season, providing an endless supply of cut flowers for the house. I am always delighted to have fresh blooms, something to brighten every room, and it's a joy to walk through the garden and choose the perfect ones for the house.

And then, there's the greenhouse. The latest addition to the estate. It's a glass sanctuary tucked beside the vegetable garden, a space where seedlings are coaxed into life, ready to be planted out into the beds when the time is right. Heirloom seedlings—tomatoes, peppers, lettuce, and so much more—are nurtured here. It's also home to plants that wouldn't survive the harsh winters outside: figs, lemons, limes, kumquats, pelargoniums, agapanthus, and agaves. These plants travel from the greenhouse to their spots throughout the property, creating little surprises of green and color wherever they land. Many of them are culinary treasures, adding zest and flavor to the meals prepared from the garden's bounty.

The surrounding meadow has become a crucial part of the ecosystem. It feeds the honeybees that are carefully kept on the property. The meadow is rich with nectar and pollen, providing a haven for the bees and other insects that are essential for the garden's health. The bees, busy as ever, swarm the Braeburn apple trees that stand just behind the vegetable garden each spring. I watch them with fascination as they hover around the blossoms, a blur of wings and movement. When they swarm, they are carefully moved to their hives, where they produce honey that I use for everything from tea to baking.

The orchard, too, plays its part in the life of the garden. The Braeburn apple trees are a sight to behold, their branches heavy with fruit every year. Originally, four hundred apple trees were planted on the property, forming the foundation of this orchard. The rows of apples have become a food source for not only the bees but also for myself. Grid food-shape pruning was used to encourage even growth, making the orchard not just productive but beautiful, as the trees form neat, orderly lines against the landscape.

In a way, the vegetable garden is a reflection of the farm itself—rooted in history, yet constantly evolving. It's a place where food and beauty intertwine, where plants grow with intention, and where every corner offers a lesson in patience, hard work, and reward. From the hedge that marks its borders to the soil where everything is planted, this garden feels like a living testament to the idea that a piece of land can be nurtured and made to thrive once again. It's a space that continues to breathe, grow, and change, just as the seasons do. And I am honored to be part of its story.

Left: An overview of the the vegetable garden's layout. The garden is fully enclosed by yew hedges to keep the deer out.

Following pages: An aerial view of the complete vegetable garden, showing how the upper row of beds relates to the shaping of the boundary hedges.

Previous pages: As well as berries and cut flowers, the productive garden has beds dedicated to herbs.

Left: Perennial rhubarb, which I let go to seed simply to admire its candelabra-like flower spikes.

Right, above: Everbearing raspberries.

Right, below: Young lettuces planted in rows by type.

Opposite: The rounded blossoms of chives, above, and society garlic, below, make it apparent they're both members of the Allium family.

Right: I find poetry in the forms of even the simplest plants, such as this newly planted onion.

Overleaf: A mass planting of white society garlic proves that productive gardens can also have great ornamental value.

Pages 180–81: I plant many varieties and colors of dahlias, and look so forward to late summer, when they come into their own.

Opposite, above: Many of the rows in the garden are planted with a variety of dahlias.

Opposite, below: Pots of mint and "wallpaper" of dahlias make this quiet seating area one of the most pleasant places to pass a summer afternoon.

Above: Dahlias of all color ranges allow for a variety of spontaneous cut-flower arrangements.

Above, left: *Dahlia* 'Cornel' is known for its ball-shaped blooms and long vase life.

Above, Right: A tight dahlia bud promises a riot of magenta soon.

Opposite: I am so appreciative of breeders who have created so many dahlia varieties, from intense solid colors to this, tinged with the most delicate pink.

Previous pages: High hedges offer the promise of secluded conversations for this seating area.

Right: Even in winter, the vegetable garden offers sculptural moments, provided not least by a giant weeping cherry that anchors one corner.

Braeburn apples grow just outside the vegetable garden; the property was once home to an orchard that included hundreds of trees.

Left and above: I've reconciled myself to the fact that the lowest limbs of these Braeburn apples will always be slightly browsed by deer, and try to admire the strength apparent in their bare branches.

Soft meadow grasses drive circulation down the mown path; the waving grasses are juxtaposed against the clipped form of the *Carpinus betulus* hedge.

LAYERING

One of the most vital lessons I've learned in creating my garden is the concept of layering. It's not just about adding more plants—it's about weaving them together in a way that creates depth, texture, and a richer visual experience. Every layer has a purpose, from the delicate ground covers at your feet to the towering trees that reach for the sky. Together, they form a dynamic, living tapestry, each thread playing its part in a larger, harmonious whole.

My favorite view on the property is across the main lawn, where I can see how the layers of the garden unfold in a symphony of form and texture. The vase-shaped silhouettes of the *Cornus kousa* dogwoods create a striking focal point in the distance, their branches arching gracefully into the air. Their clean, elegant form contrasts beautifully with the trained crown of the *Malus domestica*, which stands like a sculpted piece of art. The towering, weeping branches of the *Prunus subhirtella* bring an element of soft grandeur, while the broad, spreading canopy of the *Quercus palustris* offers a sense of strength and permanence. Interspersed among these trees is the delicate, branching form of the *Ulmus americana*, its large vase shape adding a layer of grace and fluidity to the scene. Not to be overlooked, the upright form of the *Nyssa sylvatica* stands tall and proud, its leaves offering a bold, vertical contrast to the other, more horizontally spreading forms. Finally, the deep purple foliage of the *Acer platanoides* 'Crimson King' breaks up the scene with its rich, dark hues, grounding the whole composition.

As I look across this landscape, I reflect that the beauty lies not just in the forms of the individual trees, but in how their shapes and textures work together. The different silhouettes—the rounded, the upright, the spreading, and the weeping—create an ever-changing visual rhythm. It's a balance of form, with each tree serving a distinct purpose, while also contributing to the whole. The contrasts in size, shape, and texture create a layered effect that draws the eye in and encourages visual exploration, yet the trees are arranged in a way that feels intentional and cohesive.

But trees alone do not make a garden. To truly create balance, the mid-layer of shrubbery is essential. Shrubs play a vital role in filling in the space between the towering trees and the ground cover, adding depth and variety. Some shrubs I allow to grow in their natural forms, letting them fill out and define their own space. Others, I shape and train into more definitive shapes to add structure and contrast. The trick is knowing when to let a plant express its wild, natural self and when to bring it into harmony with the overall design.

One of my favorite ways to create this balance is with hedging. A long, horizontal hedge—perhaps boxwood or yew—creates a strong, linear presence in the garden. It serves as a natural divider, marking the boundaries of different spaces. But it's the interruption of a singular vertical tree that brings life to this otherwise straight line. Whether it's a slender birch or a columnar oak, the upright form of a tree breaks up the monotony of the hedge and adds a vertical element to the scene, drawing the eye upward and giving the garden a sense of movement. The combination of a horizontal plane balanced with a vertical punctuation mark creates a visual rhythm that's both calming and intriguing.

There's also something wonderfully grounding about a simple, all-green hedged room. While it may seem plain at first glance, it offers a much-needed pause in the landscape. It's like a palate cleanser in a multicourse meal—something to give the eye a moment of rest before moving on to the next area of interest. But as much as I love the simplicity of a monochrome hedge, it needs to be balanced with spaces that offer more variety. Without that contrast, the garden can become monotonous, lacking the intrigue that diversity brings.

Vertical layering is also essential, and this is where vines come into play. Vines add another dimension to the garden, offering the opportunity to soften hard edges, create vertical interest, or add a touch of mystery. I love the way climbing roses, clematis, or even ivy can transform a plain stone wall or a weathered trellis. They can soften the lines of a structure,

Opposite: The expressively reaching branches of a tupelo tree (*Nyssa sylvatica*) overhang square boxwood (*Buxus sempervirens*) hedges.

draping over it like a veil, or they can add texture to the garden as they wind their way up trees or fences. In certain corners of my garden, the vines create a sense of enclosure, making those spaces feel more intimate, as though the garden is inviting you in to explore.

Layering is not just a technique for creating visual beauty; it's also essential for a garden's ecological health. A well-layered garden supports a wide variety of plant life, which in turn attracts a host of wildlife. The varying heights of plants provide different habitats for birds, insects, and small mammals, while the diversity of foliage ensures that the garden stays lively throughout the year. The ground cover may offer shelter for insects and small creatures, while taller plants provide perches for birds. By layering the garden in this way, I've created a thriving ecosystem where each layer interacts with the others, ensuring that sunlight, water, and nutrients are shared efficiently.

A multilayered design also helps to ensure that no space is wasted. The ground level is as important as the vertical elements, and by filling the space with diverse plant life, I encourage a healthy flow of resources across the garden. The soil at the bottom, rich with organic matter, supports the roots of the plants, while the taller trees and shrubs create shade, protect from wind, and provide shelter for wildlife. The layering creates a microclimate where every plant can thrive.

Ultimately, layering is not just about creating beauty—it's about building a garden that's sustainable, resilient, and harmonious with nature. The layers of form, texture, and color, whether in the trees, shrubs, or vines, work together to create a garden that's not only visually dynamic but also ecologically vital. Each plant, whether towering or creeping, serves its purpose, creating a space that's greater than the sum of its parts. It's a garden that can be experienced in layers, just as life itself unfolds in layers, each more beautiful than the last.

Opposite: A deciduous *Rhododendron mucronulatum* 'Cornell Pink' anchors a corner of the pool garden.

Overleaf: A variety of tree forms add interest to the landscape, from the vase shape of *Cornus kousa*, to the weeping form of *Prunus subhirtella* and the rounded form of *Acer platanoides*.

Pages 202–203: It's fortunate to have so many mature trees on the property; being a good steward of their lives has been both an education and a privilege.

I'm pleased that the diversity of planting here supports and helps a wide variety of wildlife to enjoy the garden, even these wild turkeys.

CHAPTER SEVEN

THE POOL GARDEN

The moment I step down into the pool garden, there's a sense of entering a different world, one where everything slows and takes on a sense of purpose. The pool itself is modest by modern standards—only 12 feet by 24 feet—but this offers a feeling of intimacy. It's small, but that's part of its charm. There's something about its scaled-down proportions that make it feel like a private oasis, nestled into the landscape as though it's always belonged here.

What makes this pool garden even more special is its relationship to the history of the site. Just a few steps away sits the original gamecock house, which I've repurposed into a pool house and outdoor dining pavilion. The gamecock house, once a folly of sorts, now feels like a wise, weathered companion for the pool. Its axis aligns perfectly with a sympathetic addition to the home, pulling the eye back to the main residence while grounding the pool in the garden.

The relationship between the two buildings is significant—not just in terms of visual alignment, but also the feeling of connection between the old and the new. The gamecock house might have once been a structure with a different function, but now it serves as the perfect backdrop for outdoor dining, shaded by the massive elm tree that stands proudly nearby. It feels like an invitation to linger, to sit under the dappled sunlight, and enjoy the serenity of the surroundings.

The design is simple, but it's the details that give it its magic. The pool's three-inch thick rock-face coping borders it with understated elegance. The stone is rugged but not imposing, a perfect counterpoint to the smooth surface of the water. Surrounding three sides of the pool is a lush carpet of lawn, providing an open, airy space that contrasts with the more intimate, enclosed feeling the stone wall offers.

Right: A view of the pool garden from the upper terrace.

The wall itself, made of Byram Black stone, wraps around the garden, providing both structure and a sense of protection. It feels like a secret garden, a place tucked away from the rest of the world. White flowering wisteria climbs and drapes over the stone wall, creating a soft cascade of blooms that complement the stone's dark, rich tones. The wisteria is a sensory delight, its sweet fragrance filling the air in the spring and summer months, adding yet another layer of serenity to this garden.

One of my favorite moments in this space comes from the Gaze Burvill bench, which sits axially from the gamecock house. It faces the pool, offering a perfect place to sit and take in the view. The bench is made of oak, its simple lines adding a sense of calm, and it's framed by a backdrop of honeysuckle, 'Zephirine Drouhin' roses, and pale blue clematis. These plants seem to dance with the seasons—the honeysuckle's early blooms filling the air with sweetness, the climbing roses offering their dramatic, romantic blooms, and the clematis adding a soft, delicate touch with its pale blue flowers. Each plant seems to complement the others, creating a tapestry of color and fragrance that wraps around the bench like a comforting embrace.

What I love most about this garden is the feeling of protection it provides. It's tucked down from the main level of the house, which gives it an almost hidden quality. The walls of stone and the gamecock house frame it in such a way that it feels cocooned, a place apart from the everyday. The elm tree, which stands as a sentinel at one end of the garden, casts dappled shadows over the pool, providing moments of respite from the sun and adding to the feeling of being sheltered within nature.

This sense of protection is important—it makes the space feel like an escape, a retreat within the larger landscape. It encourages you to slow down, to pause, and to take in the beauty of the space. Whether I'm sitting on the bench with a cup of tea in the morning or enjoying a meal outdoors with friends in the evening, the pool garden offers a sense of stillness, of being completely in the moment. It's a place where the world feels a little quieter, and time itself seems to slow, if only for a little while.

The careful balance of stone, water, and plant life, along with the historical significance of the gamecock house, makes this pool garden not just a place for swimming, but a true sanctuary. It embodies everything I love about garden design—thoughtful placement, historical context, and the way nature and architecture can work together to create something timeless. Here, in this small, protected space, I've found a place that feels both intimate and open, peaceful yet full of life. And for that, it will always be one of my favorite spots in the entire garden.

Left: I overwinter pots of agapanthus in the greenhouse, then move them here to mark the four corners of the pool in summer.

The pool and main staircase are aligned with the family room, inviting visitors to step directly out onto this part of the lawn that surrounds the pool.

Opposite: A view from inside the original gamecock house, now converted into an outdoor dining room.

Right, above: A view of the gamecock house from across the pool.

Right, below: A low stone wall surrounds the pool garden, keeping it from feeling too exposed while allowing views out and across to other areas of the property—and up to the tree canopy.

This view of the pool garden reveals how it was worked to be set unobtrusively into the larger landscape.

Above: An agapanthus collection, in terra-cotta pots, lines the main staircase down to the pool.

Opposite: The trough garden and the espaliered linden trees, as seen from the pool garden.

Overleaf: An aerial view of the property. It includes a full mix of hedging, various forms and sizes of trees, outdoor garden rooms, and sculpted hedges to make a series of spaces with distinct functions.

JUXTAPOSITION

Gardens, in their most meaningful forms, are dynamic compositions—ever-changing and filled with contrasts that play off one another. When I design or tend to a garden, I think of it as a canvas, one where each element, each plant, each pathway, and each shadow tells a story. A key component of these stories, and what elevates the experience of a garden, are the juxtapositions that naturally arise within it. These contrasts, whether created intentionally or simply discovered as time moves forward, provide both tension and harmony, balance and excitement. In exploring these juxtapositions, we find the true heart of the garden.

The sense of compression and expansion is one of the most powerful tools in creating interest in a garden. Compression occurs when a space feels contained, like a tightly packed bed of flowers or a narrow, winding path. These areas invite a sense of intimacy, making the garden feel cozy and inviting. As you move through these spaces, the feeling of being enclosed heightens your awareness of every detail—the fragrance of the flowers, the rustling of the leaves, the texture of the ground beneath your feet. There's a kind of quiet energy in compression.

On the flip side, expansion is achieved by including wide lawns, long vistas, or towering trees that encourage the eye to wander. Expansive areas give a sense of freedom and openness, encouraging a deeper breath, a broader perspective. In designing a garden, I strive to create moments of both compression and expansion. Moving from one to the other creates a physical and emotional journey, where you go from a moment of closeness and focus into one of freedom and possibility.

Few things are as captivating in a garden as the dance between light and shade. Light is like a brushstroke that brings color and texture to life, casting everything in a vibrant hue. It highlights form, shapes silhouettes, and allows us to see the subtleties of leaves and flowers. Light is the most dramatic, expressive force in the garden.

Shade, on the other hand, provides a soft counterpoint to light. It cools the space, offering refuge from the sun and inviting us to pause, reflect, and rest. Shade can be mysterious, turning a corner into a quiet sanctuary where the colors of the garden seem to deepen. The play between the two is constant, shifting with the time of day, with the seasons, and with the movement of clouds. A garden that manipulates light and shade creates an atmosphere of transformation. It invites exploration, revealing new details and changing the mood with every passing moment.

Gardens are, in many ways, a symphony of silence and noise. Silence, in a garden, is not emptiness. It's the stillness of a moment, the calm that envelops you when you step into a space full of nature's presence. The rustling of leaves, the buzz of a distant bee, the sound of water trickling from a fountain—these are sounds that complement the silence. It's a silence that speaks, a space where each sound feels more pronounced because of the quietness surrounding it.

On the opposite end, noise in a garden can come from the chatter of birds, the rustling of wind through tall grasses, or the rhythmic hum of insects. Sometimes, noise can even come from human activity—laughter on a warm summer evening or the sound of footsteps across a gravel path. There's an energy in these sounds, a vibrancy that reminds us of life in motion. The juxtaposition between these silences and noises gives the garden its heartbeat, a rhythm that shifts depending on the time of day or the season.

One of the most striking juxtapositions in a garden lies in the interplay between monochromatic schemes and vibrant color. Monochromatic gardens, those with shades of a single color, can feel serene, almost meditative. A bed of white flowers, with their subtle variations in texture and form, creates a calm and cohesive look. These spaces feel organized, controlled, and tranquil, each plant enhancing the simplicity of the others.

In contrast, color—bold, bright, and often contrasting—creates drama. I love working with the vibrancy of reds,

Opposite: Soft no-mow fescue grass makes a striking contrast when planted directly against crisp *Buxus sempervirens* hedging.

yellows, purples, and oranges, but it's how they interact with the surrounding colors that matters most. A red poppy against the green of a surrounding meadow, for example, creates a striking focal point, pulling the eye instantly. The presence of color in a garden provides excitement and movement, offering a visual pulse to the space.

Both monochromatic and colorful designs bring something valuable to the table. Where one is calming, the other is energizing. The key is in how they are used and balanced within the larger garden.

The relationship between solid and void is a fundamental aspect of garden design. A solid element could be anything from a dense hedge to a sturdy stone wall or even a thick patch of vibrant flowers. These elements create boundaries, provide structure, and give definition to the garden.

Void, on the other hand, is the space between those solid elements. It's the open area that gives the solid elements room to breathe. Voids allow us to see the patterns and shapes of the solid elements, providing contrast and perspective. Without void, a garden would feel oppressive; without solid elements, it would feel undefined.

In my gardens, I love to balance solid with void. A garden needs both to achieve a sense of openness and structure, chaos and order. These contrasts create a rhythm within the space, one that encourages movement and pause.

The juxtaposition of point and line is often found in the directionality and focus of a garden. A point is a specific focal spot—perhaps an ornate urn, a specimen tree, or a statue. Points are destinations, places where the eye naturally gravitates, offering something to hold onto within a wider landscape.

Lines, however, are the pathways that connect these points. They might be winding gravel paths or rows of hedges that direct your gaze from one place to another. Lines can create movement, guiding you through the space and making the journey feel purposeful. The interplay between point and line is dynamic, always pulling your attention to new places, encouraging exploration. A garden rich in these contrasts feels like an unfolding story—one you navigate step by step.

A great garden plays with the tension between movement and stillness. The movement might come from the gentle sway of plants in the breeze, the flutter of a bird's wings, or the motion of water flowing through a stream. Movement breathes life into the garden, making it feel organic and constantly changing.

Stillness, however, is equally important. It's found in the quiet moments—the reflection of the sky in a pond, the calm after a storm, or the pause before the breeze picks up again. Stillness allows the garden to breathe, to settle into a moment of peaceful reflection.

Opposite: Tightly clipped *Taxus baccata* 'Hicksii' hedges act almost as a picture frame that emphasizes a view of a weeping *Prunus subhirtella*.

Following pages: Visual interest is created by mingling a variety of sheared forms with decadent natural forms.

Some gardens are designed to be dynamic—constantly evolving with the seasons, always changing with the weather, or growing and maturing over time. They are a visual representation of life's fluidity, of impermanence and growth. Static elements in a garden—like stone pathways or a granite statue—anchor the space, providing a sense of stability and permanence.

A well-designed garden finds a balance between the dynamic and the static, between what is constantly shifting and what remains grounded. This creates a garden that feels both alive and timeless, full of movement but rooted in something eternal.

Finally, formal and informal design elements are at the core of many gardens. Formal gardens, with their symmetrical designs, neatly clipped hedges, and precise geometric patterns, exude order and control. They evoke a sense of grandeur, an architectural sensibility that often mirrors the structure of a house itself.

Informal gardens, however, embrace a more relaxed approach. Curved paths, naturalistic plantings, and a sense of spontaneity define informal spaces. They feel free, organic, and in tune with nature's rhythms.

The best gardens blend the two, allowing formal elements to provide structure and definition while informal spaces offer freedom and surprise. The balance between the two is key to a garden that feels both welcoming and sophisticated.

Juxtaposition in a garden is not just about contrast; it's about balance, about creating a space where every element complements the next, offering moments of tension and harmony. Through these contrasts—compression and expansion, light and shade, silence and noise, and so many others—the garden becomes a living work of art, one that invites exploration, reflection, and, ultimately, a deep connection to the natural world.

Opposite, above: A slope planted with no-mow fescue creates a modern moment.

Opposite, below: Monolithic slabs of rock-faced bluestone used to create steps are offset by the softness of the surrounding grasses.

Overleaf: Strongly geometric forms juxtaposed with wild forms provide visual and textural interest.

RESOURCES

ANNUALS, PERENNIALS, AND PLANTS

Annie's Annuals and Perennials
anniesannuals.com

Bluebird Haven Iris Garden
bluebirdhavenirisgarden.com

Bluebird Moon Dahlias
bluebirdmoon.com

Bluestone Perennials
bluestoneperennials.com

Brushwood Nursery
brushwoodnursery.com

Cricket Hill Garden
treepeony.com

Dancing Oaks Nursery
dancingoaks.com

Digging Dog Nursery
diggingdog.com

Dixondale Farms
dixondalefarms.com

Far Reaches Farm
farreachesfarm.com

Forest Farm
forestfarm.com

Gilbertie's Herbs
gilbertiesorganics.com

Gossler Farms Nursery
gosslerfarms.com

High Country Gardens
highcountrygardens.com

Issima
issimaworks.com

Kurt Bluemel
kurtbluemel.com

Missouri Wildflowers Nursery
mowildflowers.net

North Creek Nurseries
northcreeknurseries.com

Oakes Daylilies
oakesdaylilies.com

Old Dairy Nursery
olddairynursery.com

Peony's Envy
peonysenvy.com

Plant Delights Nursery
plantdelights.com

Roots & Rhizomes
rootsrhizomes.com

Sandy Mush Herb Nursery
sandymushherbs.com

Santa Cruz Dahlias
santacruzdahlias.com

Schreiner's Iris Gardens
schreinersgardens.com

Shady Oaks Nursery
shadyoaks.com

Spring Hill Nurseries
springhillnursery.com

Swan Island Dahlias
dahlias.com

White Flower Farm
whiteflowerfarm.com

TREES & SHRUBS

Broken Arrow Nursery
brokenarrownursery.ccm

Colonial Gardens
colonialgardensfairfield.com

Oliver Nurseries
olivernurseries.com

Raintree Nursery
raintreenursery.com

Stark Bro's Nurseries & Orchards
starkbros.com

Trees of Antiquity
treesofantiquity.com

TROPICALS

Geraniaceae
geraniaceae.com

Logee's
logees.com

SEEDS

American Meadows
americanmeadows.com

BakerCreek Heirloom Seeds
rareseeds.com

Chiltern's
chilternseeds.co.uk

Farmacie Isolde
farmacieisolde.com

Fedco
fedcoseeds.com

Great Dixter
greatdixter.co.uk

Gurneys Seed & Nursery
gurneys.com

John Scheepers
kitchengardenseeds.com

Johnny's Selected Seeds
johnnyseeds.com

Outside Pride
outsidepride.com

Pinetree Garden Seeds
superseeds.com

Prairie Moon Nursery
prairiemoon.com

Renee's Garden
reneesgarden.com

R.H. Shumway's
rhshumway.com

Select Seeds
selectsseeds.com

Special Plants Nursery
specialplants.net

Territorial Seed Company
territorialseed.com

Thompson & Morgan
thompson-morgan.com

Totally Tomatoes
totallytomato.com

BULBS

Colorblends
colorblends.com

John Scheepers
johnscheepers.com

K. van Bourgondien
dutchbulbs.com

Netherland Bulb Company
netherlandbulb.com

Old House Gardens
oldhousegardens.com

Van Engelen Inc.
vanengelen.com

ROSES

Antique Rose Emporium
antiqueroseemporium.com

David Austin Roses
davidaustinroses.com

Edmunds Roses
edmundsroses.com

Heirloom Roses
heirloomroses.com

High Country Roses
highcountryroses.com

Roses of Yesterday and Today
rosesofyesterday.com

POTS & ANTIQUES

Barbara Israel Garden Antiques
bi-gardenantiques.com

Ben Wolff Pottery
benwolffpottery.com

Guy Wolff Pottery
guywolff.com

Italian Terrace Collection
italian-terrace.com

J's Garden Antiques
jsgardens.co.uk

RT Facts
rtfacts.com

Snug Harbor Farm
snugharborfarm.com

Terrain
shopterrain.com

Whichford Pottery
whichfordpottery.com

GARDEN FURNITURE

Barlow Tyrie
teak.com

Gaze Burvill
gazeburvill.com

McKinnon & Harris
mckinnonharris.com

Munder Skiles
munder-skiles.com

GREENHOUSES

Alitex
alitex-greenhouses.com

MISCELLANEOUS

Arbico Organics
arbico-organics.com

PHOTOGRAPHY CREDITS

Kathryn Herman: 75 bottom, 184 left, 184 right, 185, 227 bottom

Neil Landino/Landino Photo: 2–3, 10–11, 16–17, 18–19, 20, 21, 22–23, 24–25, 26, 27, 28–29, 30–31, 32–33, 34–35, 36, 39, 40, 41, 42–43, 45, 46, 48–49, 50–51, 52 top, 52 bottom, 53, 54, 55, 56, 57 top, 57 bottom, 60, 61 top, 61 bottom, 62, 63, 64, 65, 66–67, 68, 69 top, 69 bottom, 70, 71, 72 all, 73, 74, 75 top, 76, 77, 78–79, 80–81, 82–83, 84, 87, 88–89, 90, 91, 96 top, 96 bottom, 98–99, 102–3, 104–5, 106, 107, 108–9, 110, 113, 114–15, 116–17, 120–21, 122 top, 122 bottom, 124, 125 top, 125 bottom, 126 top, 126 bottom, 127, 128–29, 130–31, 132–33, 136–37, 138 top, 138 bottom left, 138 bottom right, 140–41, 142–43, 145, 146, 148–49, 150, 151, 153, 154, 155 top, 155 bottom, 156, 157, 158–59, 160, 163, 164–65, 168, 170–71, 172–73, 174, 175 top, 175 bottom, 176 top, 176 bottom, 177, 178–79, 180–81, 182 top, 182 bottom, 183, 186–87, 188–89, 190–91, 192, 193, 194–95, 196, 199, 200–201, 202–203, 204–205, 207, 208, 210–11, 212, 213 top, 214–15, 216, 217, 218–19, 220, 223, 224–25, 227 top, 228–29

Ngoc Minh Ngo: 4, 119, 134, 139, 152, 167, 213 bottom

Courtesy Pepperidge Farm: 13 top, 13 bottom, 14 top, 14 lower left, 14 lower right

Claire Takacs: 58 left, 58 right, 59, 93, 94–95, 100–101

ACKNOWLEDGMENTS

Gardens are not created in a vacuum. They are inherited, evolved, and enriched over time—the result of countless hands, decisions, and visions layered one upon the next. I am profoundly grateful to continue nurturing and building upon a legacy that began over a century ago.

As only the third owner of this property since the 1920s, I am ever mindful of the dedication and foresight of those who came before me. Margaret and Henry Rudkin first shaped this land with intention, followed by Peg and Archie McCardell, and later Dan and Dot Magyar. Dan served as caretaker for many, many years—a quiet steward of the landscape whose intimate knowledge of the land informed his every move. I was fortunate to overlap briefly with Dan and learn from him during that time. The mature trees I now cherish were planted under their watch, a living testament to the enduring truth that to plant a garden is to believe in the future.

My own connection to the land was seeded during my childhood summers spent on my paternal grandparents' farm in Georgia. It was there that I developed an early and enduring curiosity about the natural world—one that has guided the arc of my life ever since.

My mother, Mary Caroline Fields Mullins, nurtured this sensibility in me. A devoted gardener herself, she filled my childhood in Connecticut with trips to the local nursery and the quiet ritual of making beauty bloom. Her spirit is deeply woven into who I am today, and through my work, I hope to pass her legacy along—to inspire future gardeners as she once inspired me.

I am deeply grateful for the steady encouragement and support of my father, Theodore Mullins, and my sister, Lisa Marchiano. Their belief in me has never wavered.

To the team at Rizzoli—especially Stacee Gravelle Lawrence and Susan Evans—your vision, patience, and enthusiasm made this process feel both possible and joyful.

To Peter Lyden, who introduced me to Charles Miers at Rizzoli, I am especially grateful—that introduction helped bring this book to life.

To my team at Kathryn Herman Design—you inspire me every day. Your creativity, rigor, and passion make me proud to do this work.

To James Doyle, my former business partner at Doyle Herman Design Associates, thank you for the years of shared creativity and collaboration that helped shape my professional path.

To Ferguson & Shamamian Architects and Tallman Building Company—your collaboration and craftsmanship have elevated this project in every way.

To all those who have worked tirelessly to maintain the property—your care and attention are visible in every corner of the garden. I am continually in awe of what we can accomplish together.

To the nurserymen and nurserywomen who do the hard, patient work of growing and offering plants—without you, none of this would be possible.

First published in the United States of America in 2026 by
Rizzoli International Publications, Inc.
49 West 27th Street
New York, NY 10001
www.rizzoliusa.com

Publisher: Charles Miers
Editor: Stacee Gravelle Lawrence
Design: Susan Evans, Design per se
Production Manager: Colin Hough Trapp
Managing Editor: Lynn Scrabis

ISBN: 978-0-8478-7612-9
Library of Congress Control Number: 2025941939

Printed in China
2026 2027 2028 / 10 9 8 7 6 5 4 3 2 1

The authorized representative in the EU for product safety and compliance is Mondadori Libri S.p.A., via Gian Battista Vico 42, Milan, Italy, 20123, www.mondadori.it.

Visit us online:
Instagram: @RizzoliBooks
Facebook.com/RizzoliNewYork
Youtube.com/user/RizzoliNY